# YOUR KNOWLEDGE HAS VALUE

Amir Ahmed Omer Yousif, Sami M. Sharif, Hamid Abbas Ali

# Security Architectures for Next Generation Networks

GRIN Publishing

**Bibliographic information published by the German National Library:**

The German National Library lists this publication in the National Bibliography; detailed bibliographic data are available on the Internet at http://dnb.dnb.de .

**Imprint:**

Copyright © 2014 GRIN Verlag GmbH
Print and binding: Books on Demand GmbH, Norderstedt Germany
ISBN: 978-3-656-91768-7

**This book at GRIN:**

http://www.grin.com/en/e-book/293954/security-architectures-for-next-generation-networks

**GRIN - Your knowledge has value**

Since its foundation in 1998, GRIN has specialized in publishing academic texts by students, college teachers and other academics as e-book and printed book. The website www.grin.com is an ideal platform for presenting term papers, final papers, scientific essays, dissertations and specialist books.

**Visit us on the internet:**

http://www.grin.com/

http://www.facebook.com/grincom

http://www.twitter.com/grin_com

بسم الله الرحمن الرحيم

# Security Architectures for Next Generation Networks

### Amir Ahmed Omer Yousif
High Graduate College, Ph.D. Programme
Faculty of Electrical Engineering
University of Khartoum
Khartoum – SUDAN


Ph.D Supervisor:        Ph.D CO Supervisor:
**Prof. Sami M. Sharif, UofK**   **Dr. Hamid Abbas Ali, UofK**

– – – – – – – – ◆ – – – – – – – –

مُسْتَخْلَصٌ:

هذه الورقة عباره عن توجيهات عملية بشأن توفير التدابير الأمنية للعملية المناسبة شبكات الجيل التالي
وحماية استخدام المستخدمين السليم لخدمات الاتصالات. وبالإضافة إلى التدابير الأمنية، ينبغي للشركات المقدمه
لخدمات الإتصالات إتباع المعايير اللازمه لأمن الشبكات وإتباع الطرق السليمه للإبلاغ عن الانتهاكات الأمنية.
في هذه الورقة أيضا نحن نتعلق حول الثغرات الأمنية المختلفة الموجودة في النظام القائم ويعطي الحلول الممكنة
للقضاء عليها مستقبلا. توجد مجموعه من نقاط الضعف والثغرات في شبكات الإتصالات في هذه الورقه تم
التطرق للعديد من هذه الثغرات كما تم توضيح كيفية المعالجة منها وقفل هذه الثغرات.

## Abstract:

This paper gives practical guidance on the provision of security measures for
proper operation of next generation networks (NGNs) and protection of the users'
proper use of the telecommunications services. It should be observed by all the
operators, which operate NGNs (facility based operators) or provide services with the
use of (NGN) provided by others (service based operators). In addition to the security
measures, the operators should follow the triggering criteria and reporting procedures
set out in this document for reporting security violations. Also in this paper we
concern about different security vulnerabilities found in existing system and gives
possible solutions to eliminate them. These vulnerabilities are the possibilities to forge
key messages, unauthenticated messages and Man In the Middle attack. We proposed
a secure key generation process, random number and function generation process to
eliminate these vulnerabilities

***Keywords:***NGN, PSTN, Security

1

# 1. Introduction:

Malicious traffic is becoming more prevalent because of readily available and ever more sophisticated attack tools, and motivations are becoming increasingly varied and malicious. The operators should take into account the following security objectives, namely confidentiality, integrity, and availability, when building their network and providing their services are [2]:

- Confidentiality refers to the protection of network and user data against unauthorized access, viewing, diverted or intercepted
- Integrity refers to the protection of network and user data against unauthorized modification, deletion, creation and replication
- Availability refers to the network and service provisioning to minimize downtime due to security attacks by hackers, if any.

These objectives provide a foundation upon which a more consistent and structured approach to the design, development, and implementation of network security capabilities can be constructed.

# 2. Background:

The NGN standardization work started in 2003 within ITU-T(International Telecommunication Union), and is worldwide today in various major telecom standardization bodies. The most active NGN relevant standardization bodies are ITU, ETSI, ATIS, CJK and TMF [1]. The Next Generation Mobile Networks (NGMN) initiative is a major body for mobile-specific NGN activities, which are important contributors to the 3GPP specification for NGMN.In 2003, under the name JRG-NGN (Joint Rapporteur Group on NGN), the NGN pioneer work was initiated [1]. The key study topics are:

- NGN requirements
- the general reference model
- functional requirements and architecture of the NGN
- evolution to NGN

Two fundamental recommendations on NGN are:

- Y.2001: 'General overview of NGN'.
- Y.2011: 'General principles and general reference model for next-generation networks'.

These two documents comprise the basic concept and definition of NGN. The ITU has defined the NGN as:

"A packet-based network able to provide telecommunications services and able to make use of multi broadband, QoS enabled transport technologies and in which service related functions are independent from underlying transport-related technologies. It offers unfettered access by users to different service providers. It supports generalized mobility which will allow consistent and ubiquitous provision of services to users" [1]. Figure 1 represent the NGN architectures [3]:

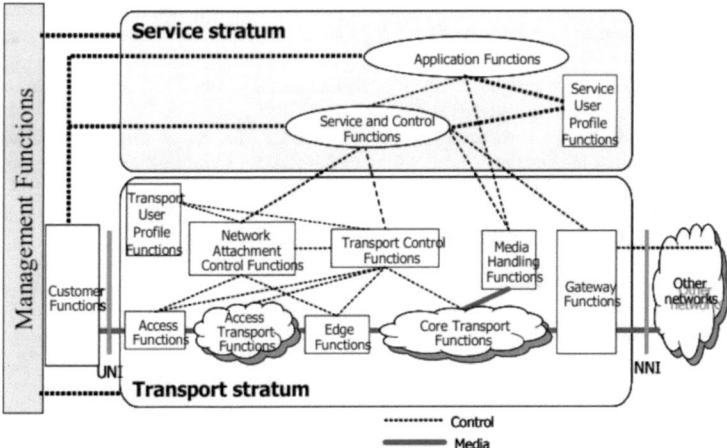

**Figure 1 NGN architectures**

*Sourse: references[3]*

## 3. Objectives:

Recognizing that security is one of the defining features of NGN, it is essential to put in place a set of standards that will guarantee, to the maximum degree possible, the security of the telecommunications infrastructure as PSTNs evolve to NGNs.

The aims of this paper is to study, understand and enhance the Security architectures for NGN networks, inorder to achieve the following objectives:

- Provide for maximal network and end-user resource protection
- Allow for highly-distributed intelligence end-to-end
- Allow for co-existence of multiple networking technologies
- Provide for end-to-end security mechanisms
- Provide for security solutions that apply over multiple administrative domains

## 4. NGN Security Architecture:

The NGN security architecture is described by the following elements:

- NGN security domains
- NGN Security services
- NGN Security protocols supporting the security services

In addition the security architecture endorses Security Gateways and renames them for the NGN application as Security Gateway Function to secure signaling and control communication among network entities.

## 4.1 Existing Security Architecture:

NGN security architecture is currently under study [4] that aim at protecting the mobile users, the data transferred and the underlying network. This architecture make the WLAN user have to execute multi-pass Authentication and Key Agreement procedure in order to get access to the IMS services. The architecture specifies three authentication steps (see Figure 2).

In the first step, the user executes the (Extensible Authentication Protocol) EAP-AKA protocol [3] to register in WLAN domain.

In the second step, the user executes the Internet Key Exchange version 2 (IKEv2) protocol [4] that encapsulates EAP-AKA, which registers him to the 3G public land mobile network (PLMN) domain.

In the third step, the user using the Session Initiation Protocol (SIP) [5] [6] executes the IMS-AKA procedure [3] for registration in the IMS domain.

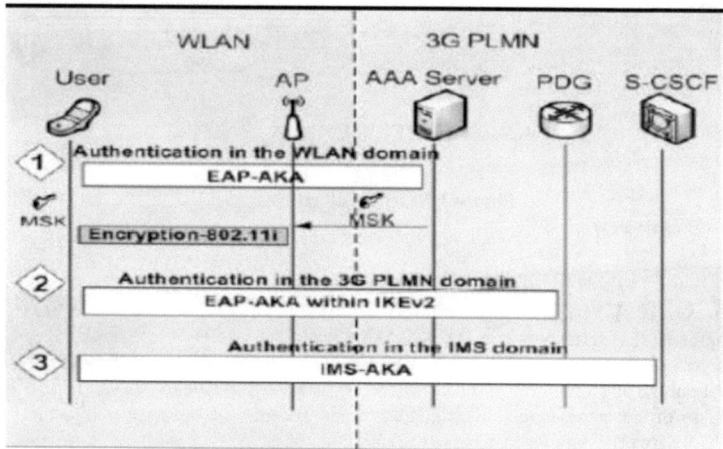

**Figure 2 Multi-pass Authentication and Key Agreement procedure for IMS service**

*Source: references [4]*

As we can see the EAP-AKA has been repeated and an execution of IMS AKA introduce an authentication overhead [5]. This overhead is related to:

- The exchange of messages that cause delays in users' authentication (i.e., especially in cases that the users are located away from their home network) and consumes radio resources and
- The computational processing that will consume the limited energy and computational resources at the mobile devices. Therefore, the aforementioned multi-pass AKA procedure deteriorates the overall system performance and may impact negatively on the quality of service offered to the end-users.

## 4.2 Security Threadof Existing System:

The main drawback of this authentication procedure is that it is vulnerable to Denial of Service attacks & Man-In-The-Middle attack. An adversary could simply send false authentication messages that the WLAN has to forward to the 3G PLMN causing overflow [4]. To remove this vulnerability requires a secure authentication process between user and PDG (Hashed based or etc) [4].

## 4.3 Security Threats Against NGN Networks:

The architecture identifies security issues that need to be addressed inorder to prevent both intentional and accidental threats.

**Destruction** – an attack on availability refers to the destruction ofinformation and/or network resources (Figure 3).

**Figure 3 Destruction Threat**

**Corruption** – an attack on integrity refers to unauthorizedtampering with an asset (Figure 4)

**Figure 4 Corruption Threat**

**Removal** – an attack on availability refers to theft, removal orloss of information and/or other resources (Figure 5)

**Figure 5 Removal Threat**

**Disclosure** – an attack on confidentiality refers to unauthorizedaccess to an asset (Figure6)

**Figure 6 Disclosure Threat**

**Interruption** – an attack on availability refers to network becomesunavailable or unusable (Figure 7)

**Figure 7 Interruption Threat**

## 4.4    Security Dimensions for Protection of NGN networks:

The security dimensions shown below outline the security protections that can be deployed to counter security threats/attacks.

1. **Access Control** – It protects against unauthorized use of network resources. Access control ensures that only authorized personnel or devices are allowed access to network elements, stored information, information flows, services and applications.
2. **Authentication** – It serves to confirm the identities of communicating entities. Authentication ensures the validity of the claimed identities of the entities participating in communication (e.g., person, device, service or application).
3. **Non-repudiation** – It provides means for preventing an individual or entity from denying having performed a particular action related to data by making available proof of various network-related actions.
4. **Data Confidentiality** – It protects data from unauthorized disclosure .Data confidentiality ensures that the data content cannot be understood by unauthorized entities.
5. **Communication Security** – It ensures that information flows only between the authorized end points. The information is not diverted or intercepted as it flows between these end points.
6. **Data Integrity** – It ensures the correctness or accuracy of data. The data is protected against unauthorized modification, deletion, creation, and replication and provides an indication of these unauthorized activities.
7. **Availability** – It ensures that there is no denial of authorized access to network elements, stored information, information flows, services and applications due to events impacting the network.
8. **Privacy** – It provides for the protection of information that might be derived from the observation of network activities.

# 5. The Results and Discussion:

NGN security architecture is in the environment of network convergence, requirements on openness increase network scales, complexity and potential security problems [4]. Users are encouraged to follow the best practices below when accessing the public telecommunications services:

- keep security patches and network interface card drivers installed on the device up-to-date
- backup all personal data on a regular basis
- make a boot disk to aid in recovering from a security breach or hard disk failure;
- install and enable personal firewall, anti-virus and anti-spyware software and keep the associated definition files and security patches up-to-date
- perform virus scan on removable disk and the files downloaded from Internet before using them
- encrypt those sensitive data stored on the device accessing public telecommunications services
- pack information or information backup in separate bag from laptop in case of theft if travelling with confidential information

- turn off the computer/notebook or disconnect from the network when not in use;
- set Internet connection default to 'manual' mode instead of 'automatic' mode;
- employ VPN technologies for enhanced end-to-end transmission protection
- use a password that is difficult to guess but easy to remember and change the password frequently
- use different sets of login names and passwords for different services
- Change the passwords on a regular basis
- report abnormal behavior to your service provider or ISP immediately
- disable Java, JavaScript, and ActiveX if possible
- disable scripting features in email programs
- disable hidden filename extensions
- do not use any device which is infected by virus/malicious code
- do not open any suspicious email and unknown email attachments
- do not store any personal or sensitive information on a computer that is shared with others
- do not cache the login name and password; and
- do not download or accept programs and contents from unknown oruntrusted sources.

## 6. Conclusion:

Focused on architectures of NGN service provision, this paper discussed existing vulnerabilities. We investigated various vulnerabilities in NGN network and give possible details to eliminate them.

Integrated, collaborative, and adaptive security in the evolving IP NGN architecture is built into the fabric of the service provider's network infrastructure and integrated with other network elements. Integration means that every element in the network incorporates security technologies and acts as a point of defense.

The IP NGN involves creation of an intelligent infrastructure from which application-aware services are securely delivered by service-aware networks. This intelligence directly benefits efforts to proactively secure networks against existing and ever-changing threats while offering service providers a major competitive advantage. The recommendations is for user to follow the best practices steps mention in results and discussion when accessing the public telecommunications services.

# References:

[1]    ITU Centres of Excellence for Europe. "Next Generation Networks - NGN".
       Available:
       http://www.hit.bme.hu/~jakab/edu/litr/NGN/Architecture/ITU_NGN_Module1.pdf

[2]    Office of the Telecommunications Authority paper. "Security Guidelines
       forNext Generation Networks". Available:
       http://tel_archives.ofca.gov.hk/zh/report-paper-guide/guidance-
       notes/guidelines-NGNs.pdf

[3]    Dr. Idir FODIL. "NGN Architectures and its Management". Available:
       http://www.networks2008.org/data/upload/file/Tutorial/T11_Fodil.pdf

[4]    A.K.M. Nazmus Sakib, Fauzia Yasmeen, Samiur Rahman, Md.Monjurul
       Islam, Prof. Dr. Md. Matiur Rahaman Mian. " Security Thread Analysis &
       Solution for NGN (Next Generation Network)" . Available:
       http://www.ijera.com/papers/Vol%201%20issue%204/AB01414491452.pdf

[5]    Office of the Telecommunications Authority. "Security Guidelines for Next
       Generation Networks" . Available:
       http://tel_archives.ofca.gov.hk/zh/report-paper-guide/guidance-notes/guidelines-
       NGNs.pdf

[6]    CISCO white paper. "IP Next-Generation Network Security for Service
       Providers". Available:
       http://www.cisco.com/c/dam/en/us/solutions/collateral/service-
       provider/secure-
       infrastructure/net_implementation_white_paper0900aecd803fcbbe.pdf

[7]    http://digilib.lib.unipi.gr/dspace/bitstream/unipi/4563/1/Tzouanopoulos.pdf

[8]    https://www.enisa.europa.eu/activities/Resilience-and-CIIP/Incidents-
       reporting/metrics/ontology/presentations/demeer

[9]    http://www.ijera.com/papers/Vol%201%20issue%204/AB01414491452.pdf